HE THORN *[Thorn]* LANGUAGE *[Ōs]*

GIFT *[Ġyfu]* JOY *[Wyn]*

HE YEW *[Ēoh]* THE GAME A

A STAR *[Tīr]* THE BIRCH *[Beorc]* THE

n] THE SEA *[Lagu]* THE GOD OF

THE DAY *[Dæg]* THE OAK *[Āc]* THE

URE *[Iar]* THE CLAY *[Ēar]* WEALTH

N *[Thorn]* LANGUAGE *[Ōs]* RIDING

yfu] JOY *[Wyn]* HAIL *[Hægl]* NEED

[Ēoh] THE GAME *[Peorth]* A WATER

[Tīr] THE BIRCH *[Beorc]* THE HORSE

A *[Lagu]* THE GOD OF FERTILITY

y *[Dæg]* THE OAK *[Āc]* THE ASH

WEALTH [Feoh]   THE WILD OX [Ūr]

RIDING [Rād]   THE TORCH [Ċēn]   T

NEED [Nȳd]   ICE [Īs]   THE YEAR [Ġēr

WATER PLANT [Eolhx]   THE SUN [Sige

HORSE [Eh]   THE HUMAN BEING

FERTILITY [Ing]   NATIVE LAND [Ēthe

ASH [Æsc]   THE BOW [Ȳr]   A SEA CR

[Feoh]   THE WILD OX [Ūr]   THE TH

[Rād]   THE TORCH [Ċēn]   THE GIFT

[Nȳd]   ICE [Īs]   THE YEAR [Ġēr]   THE

PLANT [Eolhx]   THE SUN [Sigel]   A S

[Eh]   THE HUMAN BEING [Man]   TH

[Ing]   NATIVE LAND [Ēthel]   THE

THE RUNE POEM

THE RUNE POEM

Wisdom's Fulfillment
Prophecy's Reach

TRANSLATED AND ANNOTATED

BY JIM PAUL

CHRONICLE BOOKS
SAN FRANCISCO

Library of Congress Cataloging-in-Publication Data:
Rune poem (Anglo-Saxon poem). English
    The Rune poem : wisdom's fulfillment, prophecy's reach /
    translated and annotated by Jim Paul.
        p.   cm.
    ISBN 0-8118-1136-0 (hc)
    1. Didactic poetry, English (Old)—Modernized versions.
    2. Prophecies—Poetry.   3. Runes—Poetry. I. Paul, Jim, 1950-
    II. Title.
PR1768.R83A36   1996
829'.10508—dc20   95-17625
                                                                    CIP

Book and cover design: Gretchen Scoble
Carvings of Rune Characters: Christopher Stinehour
Calligraphy: Mark Van Stone

Distributed in Canada by Raincoast Books,
8680 Cambie Street
Vancouver BC V6P 6M9

10 9 8 7 6 5 4 3 2 1

Chronicle Books
275 Fifth Street
San Francisco, CA 94103

INTRODUCTION

THE BOW, THE HORSE, THE SUN, THE SEA, AND THE POEM

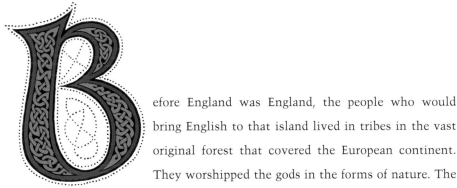

efore England was England, the people who would bring English to that island lived in tribes in the vast original forest that covered the European continent. They worshipped the gods in the forms of nature. The runes were their mystical signs, appearing in many places in that early culture as motifs on jewelry and domestic objects—clothing, tools and weapons—as symbols on boundary stones and bridges, and as letters with magical power, cast in lots for divination. The runes took on phonetic values, like ordinary alphabetical characters, and acquired secular purposes, which became more predominant as the Middle Ages proceeded. Still, their original function was to link the natural and the supernatural, the earth and the gods. In the older Germanic societies, families and tribes cast runes often, divining these symbols to learn what Fate held in store.

WRITTEN IN ENGLAND in the Middle Ages, this poem records the names and the meanings of twenty-nine runes. Manuscript evidence for the poem dates to about A.D. 1000, though the poet who wrote these verses may have lived some centuries before that. As deep into antiquity as this seems to be, the runes themselves are much deeper still, arising from a time perhaps as early as the first century, when Angles, Saxons and other tribes of Germanic warriors still roamed the mainland. By the medieval period of European history, the runes were already ancient elements, an old code shared among people of diverse northern cultures. IN THIS OLD ENGLISH POEM, we find the poet looking back, across the Channel and into those forests, to find and record these signs. He gives us this set of *characteres alphabeti peregrini,* as one eighteenth-century librarian called them: strange alphabetic characters, named for specific phenomena of that earlier time, those northern tribal people signifying by these marks the spring, the oak, the ox, the ice, and other aspects of their daily life.

BY THE TURN of the first millennium, runes were already a curiosity, the charms of country folk and the esoteric toys of monks who played with them in riddles and used them for secret codes. The runes may have come to the north more than a millennium earlier, as remnants of a letter series based on the Etruscan alphabet, which was used in Etruria until the second century B.C. when Rome conquered that sub-Alpine land. So the forms of this written language became extinct in its home region, replaced by the Roman alphabet, though these letters—brought to the north first, perhaps, by Etruscan traders—provided forms for the runes, symbols shorn completely, it appears, of any earlier alphabetical usage. IN THE LONG STARK TIME after Rome itself fell—the Eternal City looted by rune carriers in A.D. 410—these forest tribes renamed the letters, and the runes began to function as supernatural symbols, incorporated into the divine lore of the north. The runic set, which varied slightly across northern Europe, was applied to the mystical understandings of local fertility cults. By then a runic inscription on the hilt of a sword was thought to lend magical power to the warrior wielding it. Runes carved on a stick, even, might make it into a fatal wand. In legends, runes told the future, eased the pains of childbirth, even raised the dead. BEFORE THE APPEARANCE OF RUNES, the predominant symbols in northern Europe were Neolithic icons, appearing as rock carvings, representations of animals, objects, human beings, and gods from the almost inconceivably long period—relative to our own—of Europe's Stone Age. Some of the runes resemble these older symbols and seem to share their identities. In this way, the runes represent an intermediate step, standing between that Neolithic understanding and the new learning, which arrived in the form of Roman letters and Christian doctrine, brought to the north by the Church in the Middle Ages.

READING THIS POEM, we make that ancient link. A naming verse for the runes, the poem was written—or written down, anyway—around A.D. 750, by a medieval poet, probably a monk, engaged even at that early date in archaeology, preserving and explaining these old characters in his new text. He wrote out the poem not in Latin but in his daily tongue, the meaning of the runes having come down to him in that language, the vernacular Old English. WHO THIS POET WAS, when he lived and wrote, we cannot say. All we know is that his poem was rescued about two centuries later—a thousand years ago at the turn of the first millennium—when another cleric finally copied it into a manuscript that, for a time anyway, survived the general holocaust of history. That tenth-century scribe included this old poem of pagan matter—modern scholars have called it *The Rune Poem*—in a manuscript of wholly unrelated and much newer Christian material. So it survived. That manuscript, which itself no longer exists, became *The Rune Poem*'s sole link to us.

PERHAPS THE MOST POWERFUL aspect of the poem is the prospect it offers a reader at the end of the second millennium. From here we peer into a thousand years of history to find this medieval English poet, peering in his turn as deeply into his own origins. Among the runes he recorded is one for the aurochs, a ferocious forest buffalo. These wild oxen— only somewhat smaller than elephants, noted Caesar in his *Gallic Wars*— were esteemed by the folk of those ancient woodlands as their respected and powerful enemy. Never appearing in England, the aurochs survived in the forests of Central Poland until 1627. HORNS OF THE AUROCHS sometimes were made into drinking vessels. Large enough to hold a flagon of ale, such a horn often became a family heirloom, decorated with silver and marked with runes to protect its owner from poisoning. So too the rune for the aurochs survived the centuries, prized for its magic, which partook of the power of that animal, a spirit of the original forest itself.

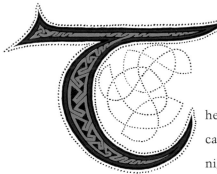

hese rune people, northern barbarians—so called by the Romans, anyway—believed that night ushered in day, as they might in the dark north. They counted their week by nights. So reports the Roman soldier and historian, Tacitus, whose ethnographic sketch, *Germania*, appeared in A.D. 98, describing these big, ferocious, blue-eyed people. They lived in rough wooden houses, set apart from one another in the forest, wrote Tacitus. Their holy places weren't temples in cities, but special groves within the deep woods. **THEY WERE A PEOPLE** of the horse, riding in the forest. "The children play at riding, the grown men compete at riding, and the old will not give it up," wrote Tacitus. The priests cared for white stallions in the sacred groves, horses "undefiled by any toil in the service of man," whom they observed for significant signs and divine omens. These priests were merely servants, the people thought. The horse was divine, a counselor to the gods themselves. **THEIR LIVES** must have been idyllic in summer and in times of peace. In winter, a family took refuge in a cave dug beneath the house, which also sheltered them when war came. In battle, they were fierce and fearless in the wild barbarian manner, each small band of men fighting to the death around its leader. The women and children accompanied the warriors to battle, to cheer them on and to tend to the wounded. The women were not above comparing their husbands' gashes to see who had fought more bravely. **THE WOMEN WORE** a tight garment of long underwear beneath linen robes marked with runes in a purple pattern. They wore no finery for walk-ing outdoors, but furs fastened with a brooch or a long thorn, cloaks that left their strong shoulders exposed. The men of the tribe, wrote Tacitus, believed that there resided in these women "an element of holiness and a gift of prophecy." "They did not scorn to ask their advice or lightly regard their replies." A GREAT SIN it was, among these people, to turn a visitor from the door. A host welcomed a guest with the best meal his means allowed, and then accompanied him to the next house, where both were welcomed with equal hospitality. When a guest went home, it was customary to give him any parting gift he desired; likewise the host might get a gift from the guest as well. THIS SOCIETY, like others in traditional culture, maintained itself by such gift giving. From chief to retainer, from retainer to chief, from husband to wife, kin to kin, stranger to stranger, such gifts held the world in balance. The runes, too, were part of this process, honoring the gifts of the gods. Carved on doorposts and daily objects, woven into cloth or traced upon the earth, the runes paid constant homage, returning the gift of power from the stars, the trees, the animals, and the other forms and creatures they represented.

TACITUS DESCRIBED A FIRST-CENTURY Germanic ceremony of casting runes for augury—for telling the future. The branch of a fruit-bearing tree was sliced into thin sticks, each carved with a single rune. These ballots were scattered at random on a white linen cloth, and the priest—his red hair top-knotted, his beard long—lifted his eyes to the sky and let his hands find three of the sticks. The runes might forbid a reading on that occasion, but if they appeared favorable, the combined meanings of the figures thus randomly selected provided a basis for actions in the future. After reading the runes, wrote Tacitus, the priests went into the forest to the sacred groves and observed the divine white stallions for confirming signs.

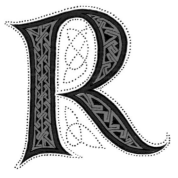unes seem designed to be carved into wood—their transverse elements are cut at forty-five-degree angles, so as to distinguish those marks from the grain when the uprights were cut across it. Many wooden runes must have been lost to us over time, but we find them across northern Europe on ancient objects of metal, stone, and bone, as well as wood, on gravestones and gold medallions in Sweden, on a silver brooch in France, on a granite pillar in Slovenia. NAMED FOR ITS INITIAL LETTERS—like *alpha-*

bet for *alpha, beta,* etcetera—the Old English rune order is called the *futhark,* after the phonetic values of its first six symbols—feoh, ūr, thorn, ōs, rād, čēn—this sequence itself considered supernaturally potent in pre-Christian times. The futhark appears, like our Roman letters, to have been derived ultimately from the Hebrew or North Semitic consonant series, and, as was noted above, reached the north around the second century B.C.

THE PREDOMINANT EARLY USES OF THE RUNES were enigmatic, "essentially private," "very brief, often cryptic, and sometimes even untranslatable," writes Maureen Halsall, the editor of the authoritative critical edition of *The Rune Poem.* "Many early runic inscriptions," Halsall adds, "show astonishingly little concern to instruct the passing reader." SOMETIMES THESE RUNES seem to have been used in more or less mundane ways—as special marks to denote a boundary, for instance, or to identify an owner. Halsall cites the instance of a runic sequence written as part of a love letter, carved on a stick and carried across the seas, the spell of the runes serving to convince the lady of the sincerity of the sender's faith. ʙᴜᴛ ᴍᴏsᴛ ᴏғᴛᴇɴ the runes functioned in an occult context, as divine symbols possessing hidden power. The term *rune* means secret, a simplification of *runstæf*, 'secret letter.' As such, rune shares its roots with the words for private consultation, for whisper and for divine mystery. Many runes have been found buried in tombs, there not for the eyes of the living, obviously, but to communicate with the spirits of the dead. ᴛʜᴏᴜɢʜ the function of the runes was supernatural, the early Germanic people named them for aspects of nature. Among its other virtues, this poem holds great interest as a material description of their environment. Through the runes, we see the world in which these people lived. The poem tells us which noxious plants they avoided, which tree's wood made the best boat. In this work we witness their love of horses, their wonder at the stars, their fear of storms at sea, their gratitude for the sun and the spring, and their dread of the clay, which took them at death. The runes hark back as well to the gods and goddesses of their forest and to their ideals of community life—to gift-giving, for instance, and to patience in times of need.

WHEN CHRISTIANITY CAME TO THE NORTH, the Church did not hesitate to use the runes as a way of making the new doctrines seem familiar to a converted people. "It is doubtless impossible to cut out everything at once from their stubborn minds," wrote Pope Gregory to the English abbot Mellitus. So the Church adopted the futhark for its purposes. In fact, the Germanic verbs for interpreting the runes became the Modern English words for understanding and producing text in general—"to read" and "to write." Despite this early use of runes by the Church, they remained in many northern places as references to pre-Christian gods and rituals, and eventually had to be suppressed. Halsall notes that, as late as the seventeenth century in Iceland, a person caught in possession of runic inscriptions might be burned at the stake. BY THEN the new system of belief had long been instituted in the north. In their day, though, the runes were seen as powerful charms, gifts from the gods. As Prometheus was said to have been tormented for bringing divine fire to earth, so the Norse god, Odin, was said to have suffered, pierced by a spear and hanging for nine nights upon the Tree of the World, to bring the runes to humanity. "I peered down," sings Odin in the Eddic saga *Hávamál*, "I took up runes—howling I took them up—and then fell back."

eorge Hickes, a bewigged antiquarian in the age of Newton, published *The Rune Poem* in his *Thesaurus* in 1705. Hickes's work is not just the best but the only source we have for the work now. Scribbled on a piece of vellum about the year 1000, *The Rune Poem* survived until Hickes's day in a medieval manuscript, incongruously bound between a collection of short penitential texts and a life of Saint Margaret—two Christian works typical of the manuscript as a whole. So the poem reached 1731 intact, its manuscript kept in London in the Cottonian collection in the British Museum and catalogued as Otho B-X (for the tenth book on shelf B of the "Otho" bookcase—each bookcase in the Cottonian was named for the Roman Emperor whose bust was placed atop it). Luckily for us, Hickes had alerted a friend, the paleographer Humphrey Wanley, to copy any references to runes he found as he read in the Cottonian. Wanley copied a bundle of material, marked it *"Alphabetica runica diversa,"* and sent it to Hickes, who was on a mission to prove Danish influence in Old English Literature. Hickes published the work in 1705—mistakenly as it turned out, the poem not being Danish—placing in his twenty-second chapter the entire text of *The Rune Poem.* Whether Hickes's printer made an accurate plate of Wanley's drawing of the manuscript page, we cannot know, as neither the drawing nor the manuscript itself exists for comparison. Wanley's was lost, and the Cottonian manuscript destroyed. The collection was housed in the all-too-aptly named Ashburnham House, which caught fire in 1731, burning the manuscript—the poem's last physical link to the Middle Ages—and leaving us with just Hickes and his single, printed page.

T his poem transcends the genre as we know it now, acting in its time as a social document and a repository of knowledge, as well as a work of literary art. An alphabet poem, such as "A is for Anteater, B is for Baboon," *The Rune Poem* gives us a stanza of verse—three or four lines of explanation and context—for each of the twenty-nine runes in the English set. In the verse for the rune for joy, for instance, we learn who feels joy most—the poor, the poet writes. OLD

ENGLISH POETRY usually relies upon traditional poetic formulae. As in Homer, the poem is composed both by the poet and by the age. Kemp Malone, among others, conceives of *The Rune Poem* as one expression of a traditional oral work by which the sequence and meaning of the runes was passed from generation to generation, in which case what we read here is not merely the handiwork of one poet, though there can be no doubt of his hand in it. Certainly tradition dictated the order and meanings of the runes. Rune poems exist also in Norwegian and Icelandic, and in comparing these versions, we may note formulaic similarities and gauge the degree to which this English version draws upon the long-standing meanings for the runes. In my notes here, I occasionally compare those traditions.

AS A PAGAN DOCUMENT—a material catalogue and spiritual guide for these early tribal people—and as a poem by a Christian monk, this work blends traditions that may not appear entirely compatible. Halsall notes that the runes involve subjects and concepts that were taboo for an orthodox

Christian, adding that "the poet was probably aware that runes were once used for magical purposes." THE POET SEEMS to have refrained—with one or two exceptions—from imposing the new Christian understanding of the cosmos on these older signs. Although a Christian view sometimes seems to temper the darker outlook of the Germanic tradition (in the verses on the runes for ice and need, for instance), more often the poet appears to give prominence to the pagan past. To conclude the poem, he may have selected a rune representing a wild sea creature, perhaps a sea serpent, taking it from its traditional place in the middle of the futhark. This sea creature, suggests one scholar, is the World Serpent, a primeval Norse deity. IN A POEM as old as this one, though, what seems to be the poet's intent may be simply an accident of the work's ancient transmission. The poem might not even be the work of one poet. Some later scribe may have decided to embroider these pagan elements; yet another monk to emphasize Church doctrine. In any case, there are dimensions here we can never know; as usual—with medieval literature, especially—we take some risk in assuming anything at all.

the RUNEPOEM

1. WEALTH [*Feoh*]

> Money may console you,
>
> though to get any credit
>
> you have to give it away.

THE NORWEGIAN VERSION of *The Rune Poem* is even less sanguine about wealth, noting simply that it "causes trouble among the relatives," though at heart both this and our poet's formulations warn us against selfishness. The primary position of this rune in the traditional order or futhark may indicate the primacy of this virtue in that culture sustained by generosity, the paradox of wealth articulated here strengthening all bonds between people. This rune name, *feoh*, has an original meaning as cattle or livestock and gives us its awful derivative, *fee*.

2. THE WILD OX [Ūr]

The wild and single-minded ox

swings its horns freely,

a bold being, stalking the moors.

THIS IS THE RESPECTFUL PORTRAIT of the ferocious aurochs *(Bos primigenius)*. The formulaic epithet "infamous moorstalker" is a familiar one to readers of *Beowulf*, reminiscent of the description for the monster Grendel. Hunted in pits, this bull appears here as a representative of the vast array of ice age mammals, the woolly mammoth and saber-toothed tiger among them, hunted to extinction by man and rarely occurring in the written record.

I feel, in the epithet for the ox's single-minded courage (his *anmōd)*, a shadow description of one aspect of being human, our multimindedness, which both hinders and enables us.

The mean thorn
pricks everyone,
evil to seize.

AN ANTHROPOMORPHIC DESCRIPTION of the thorn. In the Scandinavian tradition this rune means giant, one of the cruel, huge invaders who lived beyond the moors. In either case, this was a rune of misfortune.

That it might be "evil" to seize a thorn typifies the life-oriented and pleasure-based notion of good found in Anglo-Saxon culture. The dragon's treasure in *Beowulf* is not evil in itself, for instance, but in its going unshared, its rusting in disuse.

This rune persisted among Roman characters in the Middle English period, to designate a *th* sound. The rune still makes an occasional appearance, misread by moderns as a *Y*, as in "Ye Olde Shoppe."

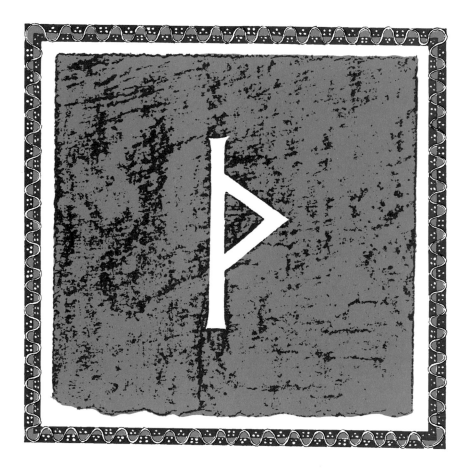

> The source of words: Os.
>
> Wisdom's fulfillment, prophecy's reach.
>
> O blessedness and hope.

THIS RUNE FOR THE SOURCE OF LANGUAGE literally means mouth, but the formulation suggests something more like divine inspiration, identified by the Greeks as the muse. To hear something surprising and wonderful out of one's own mouth is to know Os. The poet acknowledges this mystical source of language as an agency completing knowledge and extending it into the future. This rune acknowledges that language is a gift, giving it back.

5. RIDING *[Rād]*

Riding seems easy at home
though on the long road
the horse feels hard as stone.

AT HOME, we'd ride, and riding, be at home. The Icelandic *Rune Poem* is less equivocal about riding; there riding expresses "the joy of the rider." The Norwegian version, though, reads ironically as well. "Reportedly," it notes, "riding is worse for the horse."

6. THE TORCH [Čēn]

By its flame the living know the torch,

its brightness illuminating

life inside, where we rest.

IMAGES OF LIGHT suggest metaphors, though this description of the torch seems naturalistic enough. The note of luxury here—of the nobles at their ease in torchlight—recalls the small graces of that age, when work and sleep, day and vast night, were all that might be expected.

The name for this rune (čēn in Old English) gives us the modern word, keen, describing the brightness and sharpness of a knife, for instance. The other rune poem traditions identify this rune with "ulcer," an extension from "torch," perhaps, as a bodily burning, a keen pain.

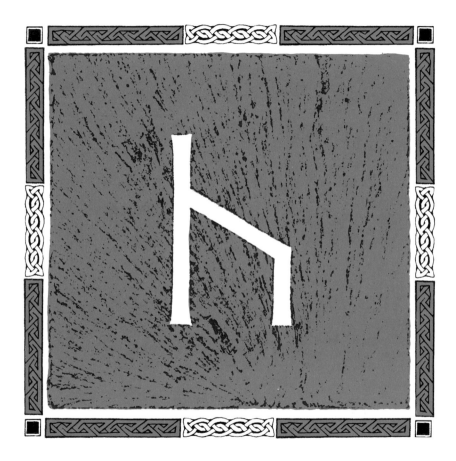

We give the gift

to us, beautiful thereby.

The exiles miss this.

IN THIS GIFT-GIVING CULTURE, the norm of reciprocity sustained everyone. The exile, outside of the giving circle, could not survive. The gift circle is a mainstay of many traditional cultures.

The figure of this rune is a diagonal intersection, symmetrical, neither horizontal nor vertical, a meeting in the middle between high and low, a fitting symbol for equal exchange. The runes for need, day, human being, and even horse seem to be variations on this one, for the gift.

8. JOY *[Wyn]*

Joy comes not to the soft,

to the untouched, complacent

with the plenty of the town.

Tᴅɪꜱ ᴄʟᴇʀɪᴄᴀʟ ᴘᴏᴇᴛ'ꜱ indirect description of joy may echo the praise of Jesus for the poor. In any case, it suggests a balance—consonant as well with the older Germanic tradition of reciprocity—between the reward to the rich of contentment and to the poor of joy.

   This rune entered Old English book hand to indicate a *w* sound.

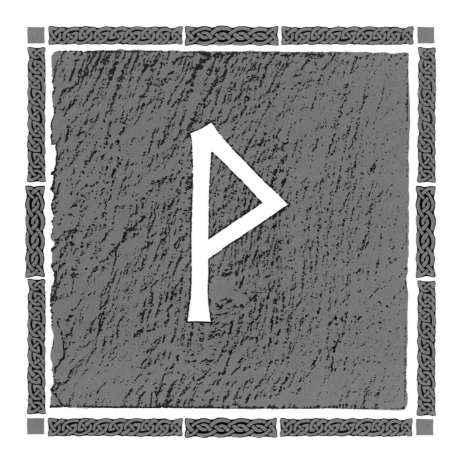

9. HAIL [*Hægl*]

Wind tossed, twisting

out of heaven, the white grains

of hail turn to water later.

THREE RUNES IN THIS POEM DENOTE WATER, in three forms:
here, as hail, later as ice and as the fluid sea. Typically an attribute of the ter-
rible winter and an ominous sign in divination, hail in this poet's description
is presented naturalistically and with an emphasis at the end on its property
of transformation. In this its presentation parallels that of the following rune,
need. In other traditions, hail is dire; the Icelandic *Rune Poem* calls it "the
sickness of serpents."

10. NEED *[Nÿd]*

Need pierces the heart,

though hope whispers here,

if we can bear to listen.

WITH THE RUNES for hail and ice, which it joins in the sequence, the rune for need poses a triad of ill omens in the casting of lots. Our poet—sanguinary perhaps in his Christian hope—tempers the tradition here, in which need appears as the worst aspect of existence, as helplessness amid suffering.

The rune for need might be an asymmetrical variation on the rune for the gift.

Cold and slick, the ice
glistens like gems,
forms a pure floor.

Tɦıs poɛт's ɒɛpıcтıoɴ oꜰ ıcɛ, like his verse on hail, is naturalistic and aesthetic, easing its harsh connotations. In the Norse tradition, Halsall
notes, "ice was the primal material from which life emerged." Perhaps we may
look back, through this rune with its grounding in the Norse genesis saga, to the
withdrawal of the glaciers after the last Ice Age some twelve thousand years ago,
the enabling moment for human habitation in northern Europe.

The new year bestows
God's extravagance of flowers
on merry and miserable alike.

UNTIL THE MODERN PERIOD, it was assumed that the new year began when winter ended, in April. In fact, the word for year in Old English referred only to the growing season, and in the various traditions this rune stood for all of its aspects, for spring, for high summer, and for harvest. This verse is one taken to be "unambiguously Christian," by Halsall, presenting the bounty of the year as an act of Christian grace, bestowed indiscriminately, regardless of its recipients' merits. This rune and the two following appear antithetical to the three previous runes, winter, hardship, and cold answered with spring, abundance, and warmth. This configuration of the rune for year is an English variation.

Firm in the earth, the yew
burns well in the fire, the joy
of the land long in the hearth.

THE EVERGREEN YEW is the first of four trees named by runes. Identified by some scholars as the type of the Norse World Tree, Yggdrasil—upon which Odin suffered to bring the runes to humanity—the yew is here treated naturalistically, its initial description quite botanical. The poet generalizes the yew's resistance, relating its firmness in the earth to its staying power in the fire. The Norwegian *Rune Poem* also praises the yew as good firewood, its sappy branches hissing in the flames.

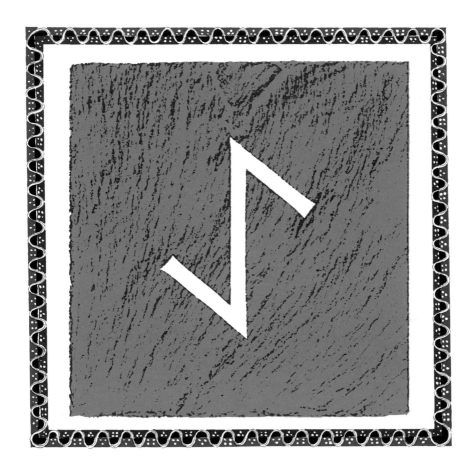

In the beerhall

the dice cup clatters.

The lucky ones laugh.

THIS VERSE is one of the poem's most obstinate. For one thing, the second line has a foot missing, the only such gap in the work, which compounds the principal difficulty, that we cannot identify this game *(Peorth)*. Scholarly suggestions range from "dice box," on which I have elaborated here, to "chess piece" or "pawn," which seems too staid, to "tune" or music, to "penis" and "apple tree," which require far-fetched translations of the rest of the verse. It's a familiar scene to readers of Old English literature, in any case, these roaring thanes at table.

15. A WATER PLANT *[Eolhx]*

> Water sprouting, fen dwelling,
>
> the cruel elksedge can cut you,
>
> can draw blood from your hand.

THIS PORTRAIT of "a kind of marsh grass upon which the elk was accustomed to sleep or browse," as Halsall notes, may be the poet's own invention. Neither the Icelandic nor the Norwegian rune poems concur in his interpretation for this archaic name, *eolhx*, which allows this poet to exercise his botanical interests and compose a verse on this sharp marsh plant, the elksedge, *eolhxsecg. Secg* means sword as well. Halsall compares the Latin *gladius* 'sword' and *gladiolus*, another sharp-leaved plant.

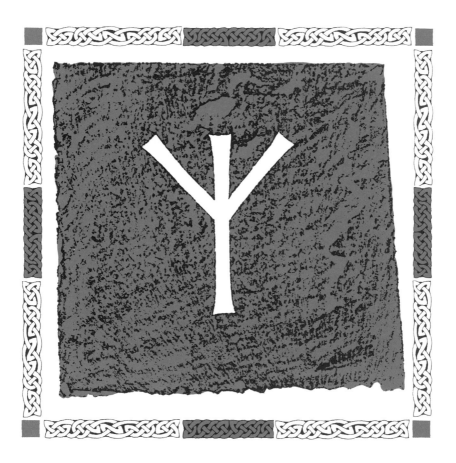

16. THE SUN [*Sigel*]

The sun is the sailor's hope.

As he rides sea horse over fish bath,

it shows him the shore.

TACITUS NOTES in his *Germania* that these northern people reckoned time by nights, a commonsense adaptation, perhaps, to so much northern dark. This verse on the sun seems to be derived from that world, its light as fleeting as hope. Ships seem not to be a favorite for this poet (see "The Sea"). In the middle line, I have retained the Old English kennings for boat and ocean.

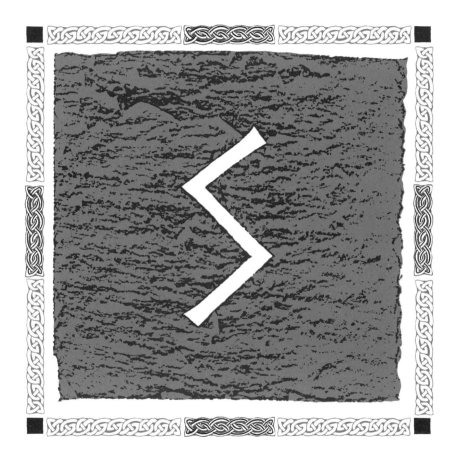

The North Star holds true,

plunging above the night clouds

on its one straight path.

THIS RUNE IS OFTEN TRANSLATED AS TIR, the name of the
Norse war god, or as Mars, the Roman equivalent, but Tir doesn't help us locate
this celestial object, and Mars is a planet, a wandering star, not holding its
course as described here. Tiw, for whom this rune was originally named, was the
supreme god of the original Germanic pantheon. Tuesday is named for Tiw, who
by the tenth century in England had become conflated with the Norse war god,
Tir. Our poet, faced with a rune naming an ancient god, takes it in a more contemporary sense as a celestial reference, as we might with Jupiter. In its time,
this rune functioned as a victory charm.

No flowers, no fruit,

yet the birch is beautiful,

its clustering leaves near the sky.

THIS LOVELY VERSE, unlike some of the others, suggests a pure appreciation of nature, apart from its possible benefit to humanity. The birch was the most numerous of the trees in the old northern forest, and the first to leaf in the spring. It played a key role in early fertility rites—perhaps because, as noted here, it had no apparent seed—and the birch-tree goddess is identified by some scholars of this period with the earth mother herself. The similarity of this rune to the English letter *B* may mean that this rune is a later addition to the runic set, influenced by the presence of the Roman alphabet.

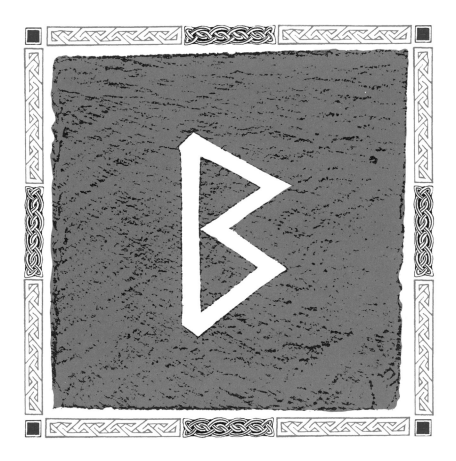

As proud of its hooves

as its rider of his words

for this wanderer's comfort, the horse.

IN ANCIENT GERMANIC CULTURE, a horse was sometimes burned on its rider's funeral pyre. They considered horses divine, though this medieval description is concrete, immediate, exact, on earth. Notice the similarity in configuration of the runes for horse and the following rune, with its elaboration of the lower transverse elements, for human being.

20. THE HUMAN BEING *[Man]*

Happy one, rejoice in life—
your friends, your poor body
by certain death betrayed.

JOY APPEARS IN ITS ANTITHESIS in this poem, and so does humanity, rejoicing in life, even in—and perhaps because of—the certain prospect of
death. Some scholars read Christian overtones in this note of life encompassed
by death, though it seems to me to be perfectly in keeping that those earlier
people, who measured time by nights, would find the light against a broader
ground of darkness. In the original, death is described as the Lord's decree,
though the reference to *Dryhten* ('Lord') may refer either to a secular or to a
heavenly ruler.

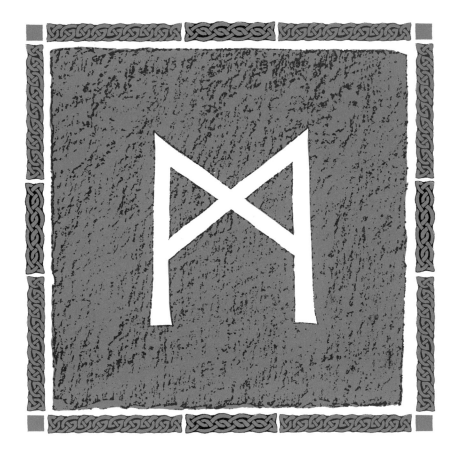

21. THE SEA [*Lagu*]

> Seasick and tired of water,
>
> then terrified as the storm-surge
>
> sweeps over the ship.

THIS IS THE RUNE FOR THE SEA, an image for chaos in which this poet finds no pleasure, depicting it as the fear it inspires in reluctant sailors. We might read this verse as the contrary to the lines for the sun, called the sailor's hope. In other runc poem traditions, water appears as less engulfing and more beautiful, as a mountain waterfall, for instance, in the Norwegian poem. Perhaps this reluctant sailor is our poet himself.

As in the previous verse, these lines on chaos and death reveal the dark heart of the poem. The work's final note harks back to this.

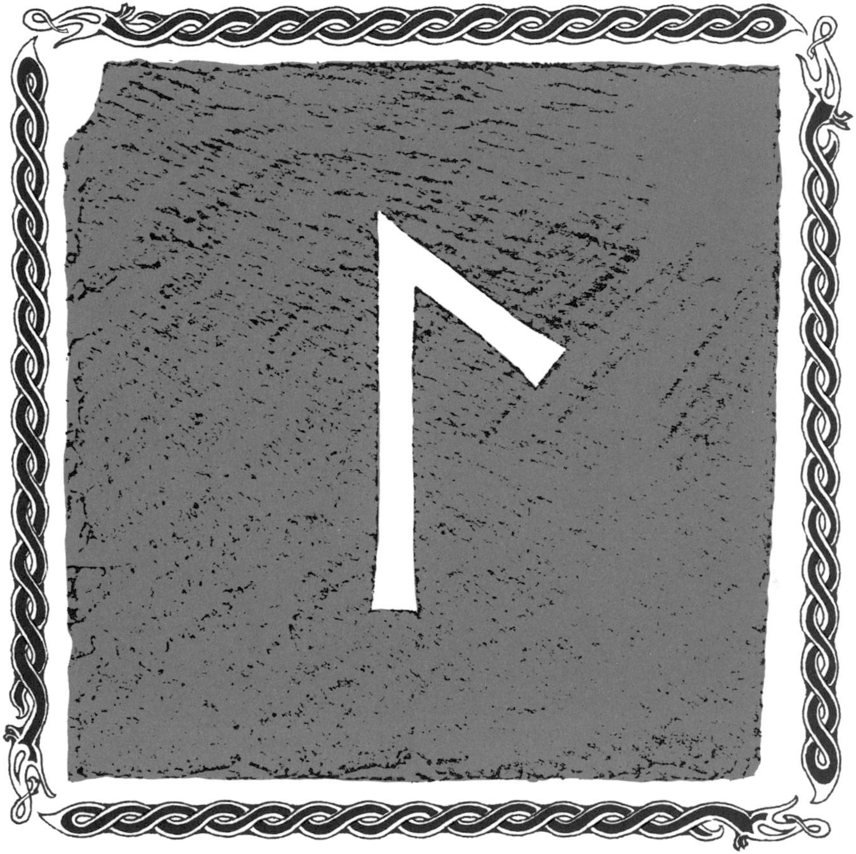

First manifest among East Danes,

Ing drove his chariot eastward

over the waves, by then so known.

ÞERE IS ÞE SOLE ÐIRECT REFERENCE in Old English literature to the early Germanic fertility god, Ing, worshipped by a people—known in antiquity as the *Ingwine,* or friends of Ing—who lived on the Baltic Sea, perhaps on Zealand Island, around the first century A.D. Ing may be one manifestation—the East Danish version—of the Germanic earth mother, Nerthus, also associated with a chariot. Kept in a sacred grove on an island, her chariot was washed once a year in a secluded lake, noted Tacitus, in which the washers themselves were afterward drowned. Ing's eastward journey may take him to Sweden, where a similar fertility god is said to be the legendary ancestor of the Swedes.

Nowadays for rights and reasons
and often for the fruits
of harvest, we love the land.

THIS RUNE FOR THE LAND traditionally ended the runic sequence, which began with the rune for cattle. By this point in the Middle Ages, the rune for cattle is interpreted in the abstract, as wealth. The land too is valued in the context of rights of ownership. I infer from this verse some purer, previous appreciation for the land's gift, the bounty of the harvest.

We love the daylight,

God's glorious illumination,

hope for rich and wretched.

Tђє CONFIGURATION of this rune for day, an oblong **x** bounded by verticals, suggests the rune for gift, though the gift rune is open ended, as if the day were the limited gift of light. The rune for human being may be derived from this one, too, though the human rune is elevated, lifted off the ground as it were, as if life were a gift, similarly limited, though in our case—in our consciousness of it, perhaps—also more remote.

The poet refers to God as *Metode* ('Creator') and so may be bringing Genesis into his poem, referring to God's creation of light. As he did in his verse for spring, the poet here emphasizes the even-handedness of such a blessing, a grace to rich and poor, noble and common alike.

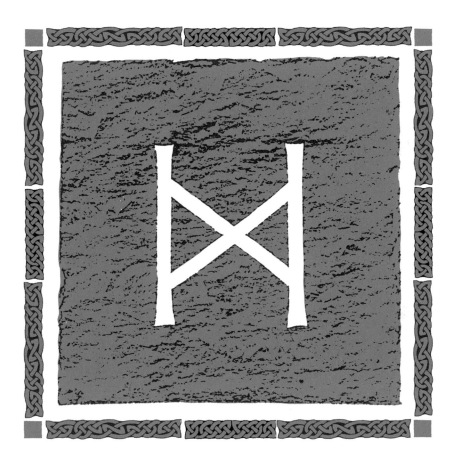

The oak is on earth for us.

Feed pigs the acorns.

Make a good boat.

THE VERSE FOR THE OAK contrasts with the verse for the birch, presenting nature in its useful aspect, as a help to humanity; the birch appeared in its autonomous existence, its beauty transcending our needs.

    This rune exists only in a later, mostly Old English tradition. Thus we might view this rune as marking the arrival—in oaken boats—of the English people themselves.

The towering ash we love,

its stout trunk steady too

amid a crowd of enemies.

Τhe ash, like the oak, is celebrated for its usefulness to people. As in the verse for the yew, the strength of the ash is generalized, though not simply to its properties in service to humanity—as the tough yew persisting in the fire—but to human beings themselves, the ash's power conveyed upon the warrior wielding it as a spear or fighting stick. The yew seems even to share our enemies. The sturdy ash is the fourth and last tree rune, after yew, birch and oak.

27. THE BOW [Ỹr]

Strapped to the horse
with the rest of the gear,
the bow, ready to go.

THIS RUNE'S MEANING has been much debated; bow is taken as its
traditional translation. If correct, it appears here in the beauty of its potential,
at the beginning of a journey. As an enabling device, the bow presents a paradox,
a thing most real in its capability, most present in some potential future.

Note the similarity here of this rune to that for the wild ox, an identifica-
tion, perhaps, of the bow with its object.

The serpent leaves the sea
to feed and dwells encircled
by water, in pure delight.

Tђє рoєт'ѕ naturalist impulse, which may have inspired him to copy the poem in the first place, is evident here. He notes this animal's feeding habits, and we might take this verse to describe an actual sea creature of some kind, though the mention of its home as a place of joy strikes a curious note for a natural description. The rune represents some mysterious amphibian. Scholars suggest an eel, a newt, or a sea serpent, among other things. I have chosen this last interpretation, allowing the verse to allude to the archetypal fertility symbol of Norse creation myth, the World Serpent, which appears as well as a motif in Neolithic pictographs.

This obscure rune appears in an unusual penultimate position—it is usually in the middle of the order. This suggests that the poet may have placed it here for literary reasons, as a climax to the poem.

29. THE CLAY *[Ēar]*

We hate the clay, the cold flesh,

the pale corpse, the fallen

flowers, the broken promise.

Tɧıs ʟast ᴠᴇʀsᴇ, naming the earth rune, caps a principal motif of the
poem. It recalls the poet's verse for the rune of the human being, whom he
depicted rejoicing for life even in the presence of death. Here he goes further,
illustrating a dark Anglo-Saxon apprehension of mortality.

Perhaps the poet chose to contrast this last grievous image of human limi-
tation *(Ēar)* with the previous verse for the sea serpent *(Īar)*, an icon for the
ongoing, transcendent, joyous, natural world.

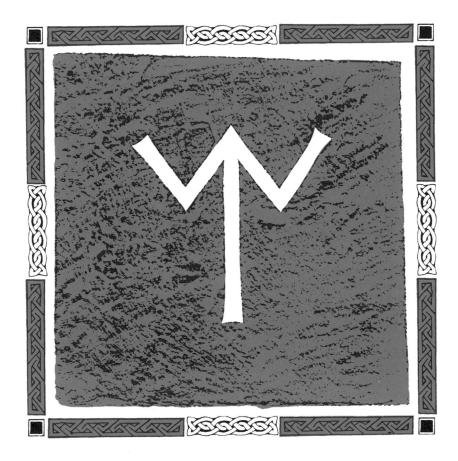

THE RUNE POEM

Money may console you,
though to get any credit
you have to give it away.

The wild and single-minded ox
swings its horns freely,
a bold being, stalking the moors.

The mean thorn
pricks everyone,
evil to seize.

The source of words: Os.
Wisdom's fulfillment, prophecy's reach.
O blessedness and hope.

Riding seems easy at home
though on the long road
the horse feels hard as stone.

By its flame the living know the torch,
its brightness illuminating
life inside, where we rest.

We give the gift
to us, beautiful thereby.
The exiles miss this.

Joy comes not to the soft,
to the untouched, complacent
with the plenty of the town.

Wind tossed, twisting
out of heaven, the white grains
of hail turn to water later.

Need pierces the heart,
though hope whispers here,
if we can bear to listen.

Cold and slick, the ice
glistens like gems,
forms a pure floor.

The new year bestows
God's extravagance of flowers
on merry and miserable alike.

Firm in the earth, the yew
burns well in the fire, the joy
of the land long in the hearth.

In the beerhall
the dice cup clatters.
The lucky ones laugh.

Water sprouting, fen dwelling,
the cruel elksedge can cut you,
can draw blood from your hand.

The sun is the sailor's hope.
As he rides sea horse over fish bath,
it shows him the shore.

The North Star holds true,
plunging above the night clouds
on its one straight path.

No flowers, no fruit,
yet the birch is beautiful,
its clustering leaves near the sky.

As proud of its hooves
as its rider of his words
for this wanderer's comfort, the horse.

Happy one, rejoice in life—
your friends, your poor body
by certain death betrayed.

Seasick and tired of water,
then terrified as the storm-surge
sweeps over the ship.

First manifest among East Danes,
Ing drove his chariot eastward
over the waves, by then so known.

Nowadays for rights and reasons
and often for the fruits
of harvest, we love the land.

We love the daylight,
God's glorious illumination,
hope for rich and wretched.

The oak is on earth for us.
Feed pigs the acorns.
Make a good boat.

The towering ash we love,
its stout trunk steady too
amid a crowd of enemies.

Strapped to the horse
with the rest of the gear,
the bow, ready to go.

The serpent leaves the sea
to feed and dwells encircled
by water, in pure delight.

We hate the clay, the cold flesh,
the pale corpse, the fallen
flowers, the broken promise.

I first translated *The Rune Poem* in the seventies, as part of my English graduate studies at the University of Michigan. My professor, the redoubtable Sherman Kuhn, presented this Anglo-Saxon work to me in purple mimeographed form, and so in the course of an ordinary assignment I found this poem, which has stayed with me since. WRITTEN IN THE HEROIC Anglo-Saxon verse style, in short lines of alliterating pairs *("Geloden leafum   lyfte getenge")*, the work felt sturdy, oaken, rough-hewn. The poem presented its naturalistic icons in particular moments, sometimes with a single gesture, the bow appearing strapped on the horse with the rest of the gear, for instance. This immediate and natural imagery, not wholly typical of extant medieval literature in general, gave the poem its staying power for me. I began working on my translation that term, and have continued to do so—there being no end to translation.

Wͻᴇɴ ɪ ᴩᴜᴃʟɪѕͻᴇᴆ ᴀɴ ɪɴɪᴛɪᴀʟ ᴠᴇʀѕɪᴏɴ in *The Seneca Review*, Professor Kuhn found it in the library and noted only, "It's rather free." This version he would probably find freer still. Perhaps it would be more prudent to treat such ancient literature simply as artifact, the poem no different from a drinking vessel of carved ox horn, for instance. I cannot do this, though, nor, I believe, can any passionate reader, some part of poetry always remaining poetry. Tͻɪѕ ɪѕ ᴏͽᴠ ʀᴇɴᴆᴇʀɪɴɢ. My impulse here has been to move toward the vernacular spirit of this work—and sometimes away from the Anglo-Saxon conventions themselves. I have favored the poem's immediacy in some of my other choices as a translator, speeding the delivery of the verse somewhat in Modern English, to enhance that immediacy and to charge the stanza with the gesture of aphorism, which is the soul of the piece. Admittedly, my models for rendering such aphorism in imagery also extend to other idioms, to the poems of Williams and Bashō, among others. As for alliteration, I have attempted here to touch that base just often enough for the contemporary reader to feel it as part of the work; so too have I treated some of the other features of Anglo-Saxon verse, such as the traditional kenning or heroic epithet.

ACKNOWLEDGMENTS

Chronicle Books granted me this return to the Middle Ages, and I would like to thank my editor Annie Barrows and everyone at Chronicle for the journey. I've also returned in this effort to medieval English studies at the University of Michigan. Thanks especially to Thomas Garbaty, emeritus professor, who read this book in draft.

Other contributors to the creation and production of this book were Leslie Jonath, Sedge Thomson, Harry Clewans, Holly Blake, Gretchen Scoble, Karen Silver, and Frances Bowles. Thanks to all, and to the editors at *The Seneca Review*, who first published my translation of this work. I'm grateful as well to my agent Chuck Verrill for his efforts.

Further acknowledgment also needs to be made here to Maureen Halsall, editor of the authoritative critical edition of *The Rune Poem* (University of Toronto Press, 1981). I recommend Halsall's volume to anyone who wishes to continue and deepen a study of this poem.

ABOUT THE AUTHOR

JIM PAUL IS A POET AND A WRITER OF CREATIVE NONFICTION.
HE HOLDS A DOCTORATE IN MEDIEVAL ENGLISH LITERATURE FROM
THE UNIVERSITY OF MICHIGAN. HIS BOOKS INCLUDE
Catapult: Harry and I Build a Siege Weapon,
What's Called Love: A Real Romance, AND
Medieval in LA: A Weekend at the Edge of the West.

IE THORN [Thorn] LANGUAGE [Ōs]

GIFT [Gyfu] JOY [Wyn] HAIL [Hægl]

HE YEW [Ēoh] THE GAME [Peorth] A

A STAR [Tīr] THE BIRCH [Beorc] THE

a] THE SEA [Lagu] THE GOD OF

THE DAY [Dæg] THE OAK [Āc] THE

URE [Iar] THE CLAY [Ēar] WEALTH

J [Thorn] LANGUAGE [Ōs] RIDING

yfu] JOY [Wyn] HAIL [Hægl] NEED

[Ēoh] THE GAME [Peorth] A WATER

[Tīr] THE BIRCH [Beorc] THE HORSE

A [Lagu] THE GOD OF FERTILITY

y [Dæg] THE OAK [Āc] THE ASH

WEALTH		THE WILD OX	
RIDING	THE TORCH		T
NEED	ICE	THE YEAR	
WATER PLANT		THE SUN	
HORSE	THE HUMAN BEING		
FERTILITY	NATIVE LAND		
ASH	THE BOW	A SEA CR	
	THE WILD OX	THE TH	
	THE TORCH	THE GIFT	
	ICE	THE YEAR	THE
PLANT	THE SUN	A S	
	THE HUMAN BEING	TH	
	NATIVE LAND	THE	